SARAH FISH

Let's Get Ready to Make Art

How to kids can create their own art studio at home.

Contents

1	Introduction	1
2	Places to Buy Art Supplies	3
3	Creating Your Own Studio	6
4	Art Supply List	9
5	Drawing and Dry Materials	14
6	Painting	20
7	Printmaking	25
8	Collage and Mixed Media	30
9	Sculpture	33
10	Art Vocabulary	38
11	Conclusion	43

1

Introduction

H ello aspiring artists, after reading this book, you will be on your journey to creating your own studio at home with a variety of materials to use. Please feel free to read it front to back or jump around based on your personal knowledge and interests. I have included places to shop, clean up procedures, art activities, art vocabulary, and more, which should give you an overview of the range of art making that can happen at home. Also, make sure you include your parents while reading the book. They may not be uncomfortable with you having certain supplies, this book may help you in making your case of why you want to create a studio space, buy $100 worth of supplies, or enroll in a specific art class. *Let's Get Ready to Make Art* is a quick resource to use as you develop your artist style.

As an art teacher, I love exposing children to various materials and processes within my art classroom. Wherever you are on your art journey, I hope this book exposes you to new ideas and materials. A few things to remember, always have an open mind when creating art. Sketch, write, and map out all of your ideas, it is the only way to get the "bad" ideas out of your brain. Once you get the bad ideas out on paper, new ideas will have room to develop. Lastly, have fun, don't take it too seriously or compare yourself to others, and be proud of your work!

2

Places to Buy Art Supplies

I have compiled a list of places to buy your art supplies along with pros and cons of each place. This is, by no means, a complete list and you may have a place in your town that you already know carries art supplies. Use this to find new materials or to compare prices.

BLICK Art Materials

This online art retailer carries over 110,000 art supplies. I like to purchase from them because the wide range of materials are available in student grade to professional grade quality. They also carry certain supplies that are hard to find at other craft stores.

Website: https://www.dickblick.com/

Amazon

The mega retailer has made so many things available at your fingertips. They are great for basic art supplies. Some items are cheaper on Amazon, such as Sharpies, where other supplies can be more expensive. For example, basket weaving supplies are more expensive on Amazon than through Blick. When purchasing art supplies from Amazon, follow the reviews and carefully read the description (that goes for most anything you buy online).

Website: https://amazon.com

Michael's, Hobby Lobby, and other arts and craft stores

These stores are great because they are convenient and you can actually browse the aisles. Maybe that is something I care more about than the younger generation but there is something about walking down an aisle and being able to pick up the item and compare it with whatever is next to it on the shelf. A downfall to these stores is that the items tend to be higher in price. Check for coupons and ask about student discounts (I get an educator discount, so maybe they have one for students, it's worth asking about).

Website: https://www.michaels.com

Website: https://www.hobbylobby.com

Target and Walmart

These big box stores do not have a large art section and shouldn't be the only place you shop. However, if you are always being dragged along on a shopping trip, make it a priority to check out their art supplies and browse the aisles. I have found random items that are useful in my studio or for mixed media artwork. Don't forget to check out the dollar bins (I go to Target and they are at the front, I don't know about Walmart, but the dollar bins always have some random things that can be used in your studio).

Website: https://www.target.com

Website: https://www.walmart.com

You Local Art Supply Store

If you live in a city, chances are high that there is a local art supply store. Being a small, independent store, they typically have higher prices but you are supporting a community business. Even if you don't regularly purchase supplies from the local store, they are worth getting to know because they often will hold classes, workshops, or just be willing to talk to you about your work and answer questions. Ceramic stores, glass studios and painting shops are just a few of the places you could check out.

3

Creating Your Own Studio

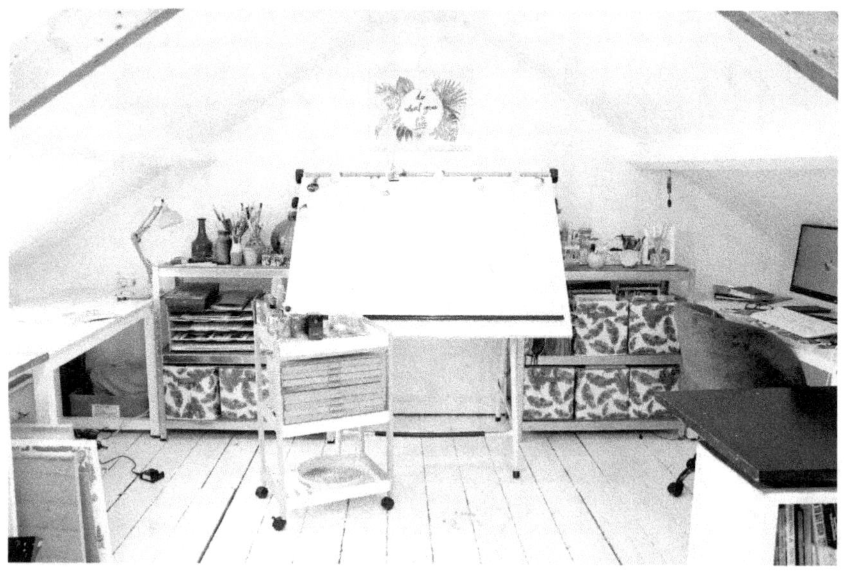

I t doesn't matter if you are transforming a corner of your bedroom into a studio space or have an entire room to use, maximizing your space for what you need it for is key. Think about what processes you like to engage in. Do you favor drawing in a sketchbook or do you like making 3-dimensional objects? Your work habits and material preferences will determine how you set up your space so it holds the supplies you will most often be using.

If you enjoy working in a sketchbook or painting small canvases, a corner of your room can transform into your studio space. If you don't have a desk that is large enough (I would recommend a tabletop that is at about 4 ft. wide), ask your parents if they would consider upgrading your smaller desk. Next, gather containers to hold various drawing materials, such as pencils, markers, paint brushes, rulers, scissors, etc. If you are on a budget, repurposed plastic containers or jars. Paints should be stored in their original containers in a large plastic bin. Go ahead and grab yourself a desk organizer to hold various papers. Command hooks or a peg board are great ways to store items off of the desktop but still be easily accessible.

Are you always building things with whatever is around? Do you not have any extra space in your bedroom? Or maybe you parents don't want certain supplies in the house. Ask if you can have a small part of the garage, basement, or shed to use as a workspace. You will still need a desk or counter top for your work area. Depending on the materials you like to use, purchase larger containers or repurposed old cardboard boxes to hold bulkier supplies.

Don't worry if the only space for you to create artwork is at the kitchen table. This should not stop you from creating, it just might make it trickier to work (because your mom will not want you to leave your half finished painting on the table all day, everyday). My best advice is to stick small in size, not in ideas. Get a rolling cart that you can load with small containers for supplies which will make cleaning up a breeze. Talk with your parents about longer periods of times you can use the table, this may be after dinner or on the weekends. You can also purchase a drawing board or lap desk so you can draw anywhere in the house.

4

Art Supply List

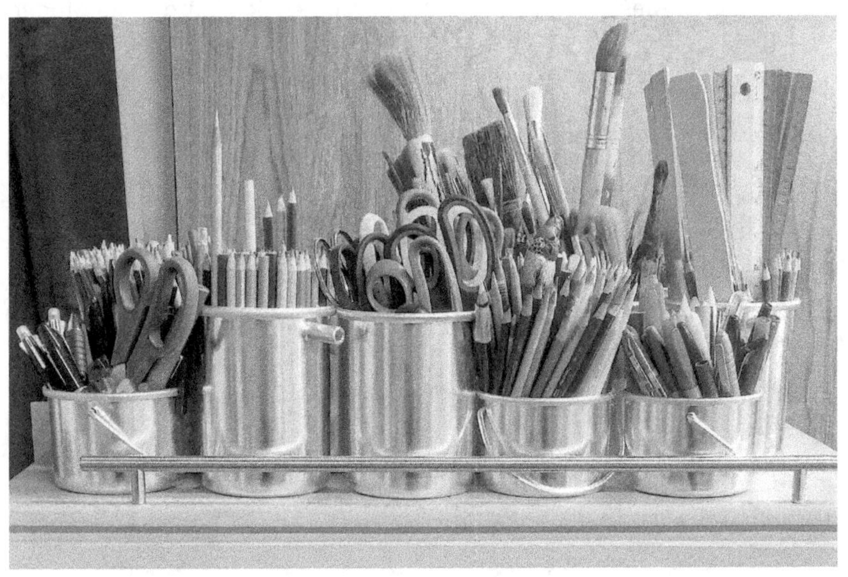

B elow is a list of supplies I recommend having on hand for various art making projects. The supplies are listed by process so you can get an idea of what you might want to buy (or have people buy you for gifts) based on your personal interests. I have also included some technique specific supplies and more advanced or expensive supplies for those who are really into a certain process.

General Supplies

- Wooden pencils
- Erasers
- Pencil Sharpeners
- 12 inch ruler (a larger size is great for those of you who like working big)
- Various adhesives - masking tape, glue stick, liquid glue, Modge Podge, hot glue
- Scissors
- Craft knife, such as X-acto knife
- Box cutter
- Cutting mat (or scrap cardboard to protect your tabletop when cutting)

Drawing Supplies

- Drawing pencil set (preferably, a set that includes 6 different ranges of harnesses)
- Stumps for blending pencil
- Drawing board for a flat surface to work on
- Compass
- Colored pencil set (preferably, at least 24 colors)
- Colorless blender
- Various markers - thin tip, chisel tip, brush tip (preferably, at least 24 colors)

- Variety of pens
- Chalk pastels
- Oil pastels
- Various papers
- Sketch paper is thinner, making it good for sketching ideas
- Drawing paper is a little thicker, good for final drawings
- Illustration paper is thick and markers will not blend through
- Various colored paper, black is a must as it makes for an awesome background for colored pencil drawings

Painting Supplies

- Tempera paint (you should have at least the primary colors, white, and black, all other colors can be mixed or you can purchase them)
- Acrylic paint (you should have at least the primary colors, white, and black, all other colors can be mixed or you can purchase them)
- Paint pens
- Watercolor palette
- Liquid watercolor paints
- Various sized paint brushes for tempera and acrylic paint – these brushes tend to be stiffer to hold a thick body paint
- Various sized paint brushes for watercolor– these brushes have softer bristles which hold the water
- Water containers (repurposed old yogurt containers or plastic cups)
- Paint brush cleaners (not necessary but good to have, I like Pink Soap as it is easily available, fairly cheap, and works well)
- Various papers and canvases
- Heavy weight paper (it should say painting paper, if the paper is not thick enough you risk it tearing or wrinkling)
- Watercolor paper (this is different than paper for tempera or acrylic

paint as it has a textured surface which holds the watercolor)
- Canvas paper
- Canvas boards
- Sketched canvases
- Paint palette (use paper plates, wax paper, repurposed take out containers, or buy a plastic paint palette)

Printmaking Supplies

- Styrofoam plates or trays (repurposed meat trays)
- Paint
- Foam roller
- Linoleum pieces, as big or as small as you want (I recommend purchasing from Blick Art Materials)
- Water soluble printing ink
- Carving tools with various tips
- Brayer (for rolling ink)
- A piece of plexi glass to roll ink on
- Medium weight paper in various colors
- Large wooden spoon or baren, used to apply press to your paper when transferring the image

Collage and Mixed Media Supplies

- Various papers
- Colored papers
- Magazines
- Tissue paper
- Decorative papers

- Various glues (which is mentioned in the general supplies category)
- Random items (below are just a few examples, you can use almost anything)
- Buttons
- Rocks
- Seashells
- Trinkets
- Scraps of fabric
- Yarn
- Repurposed cans, bottles, paper towel rolls, etc.
- Photographs
- Notes

Sculpture Supplies

- Play dough
- Model Magic
- Air dry clay
- Polymer clay
- Modeling cay
- Sculpting tools (use can also use random items that you have around your house like Popsicle sticks and toothpicks or purchase a set of various sculpting tools)
- Wire in various thicknesses
- Cardboard and/or paperboard
- Paint
- Hot glue and/or liquid glue
- Yarn
- Repurposed cans, bottles, paper towel rolls, and other random supplies that can be attached together

5

Drawing and Dry Materials

Drawing is one of the first activities we learn as a child. Even writing started out as drawn pictures. You have a range of materials to use when you want to doodle, create cartoons, or very detailed self portraits. I've included a list of materials that you should try out if you haven't already, along with activities for you to experiment with the various supplies. You can literally make art anywhere if you remember to bring a pencil or pen and the smallest of notebooks.

Pencils

A pencil is the most basic art material yet can create exquisite works of art. Wooden pencils are preferred over mechanical ones, because the graphite is softer which allows the artist to blend values together and create seamless transitions. If you want to step your shading game up a notch, purchase a set of drawing pencils. The pencils range in hardness of graphite; 6B is the softest and produces the darkest shade, 6H is the hardest and produces a lighter shade, your typical wooden pencil is 2B.

One thing to be aware of as you draw with pencil is that your hand will smudge the marks on the paper. Be conscious of starting in the upper corner opposite your drawing hand and working down the paper. Or grab a scrap sheet of paper to place between your hand and the artwork.

Colored Pencils

What to say about colored pencils, they add color to your drawn pictures. Like regular pencils, they are easy to use and have little to no clean up. I almost guarantee that you have a collection of Crayola color pencils somewhere in your house. However, it is worth spending a little more money on high quality colored pencils.

Quality colored pencils, like Prismacolor or Blick's comparable options, are super smooth to use and blend together seamlessly. Plus, you can use a colorless blender to further smooth transitions. You use the colorless blender by coloring on top of your drawing to blend the colors together. Sorry Crayola, but you cannot do that with their colored pencils.

Markers

Oh, the wide world of various markers. You have washable markers, permanent markers, alcohol based markers, even fabric markers. That's not including the various tip shapes and sizes; thin tip, fine tip, brush tip. It is best to have a range of tip shapes and sizes, allowing you to create various mark qualities. Washable markers and permanent markers have their purpose and are great for simple crafts. Alcohol based art markers are an investment you might want to make if you enjoy creating colorful illustrations. Many of these markers can be refilled, so you don't have to continuously buy new marker sets every time a color runs out.

Pens

Pens are a great addition to your dry materials. They can be used with pencils, colored pencils, and markers. Various sizes of tips allow you to create a range of thicknesses in your drawing. Ink pens, felt tip pens, ballpoint pens, and gel pens are a few different types of pens to explore.

Pastels

Pastels tend to be a love them or hate them material. Chalk and oil are two types of pastels. Both are great for blending and creating soft changes of color. However, they are not great for very detailed work as they tend to be thick pieces with a blunt end. You can sharpen the pastels using a large pencil sharpener or ask your parents to show you how to sharpen it with a craft knife. Chalk pastels are, by far, the messiest material so far discussed as they produce dust as you draw. However, they are still fairly easy to clean up with water.

Clean Up

There is not much set up or clean up with the dry materials listed above. Use a damp rag, cleaning wipes, or cleaning spray to wipe down the area after your art session.

Suggested Activities to Enhance Your Drawing Skills

- Practice creating various values with pencil, whether you have one pencil or a range of pencils from a drawing set.

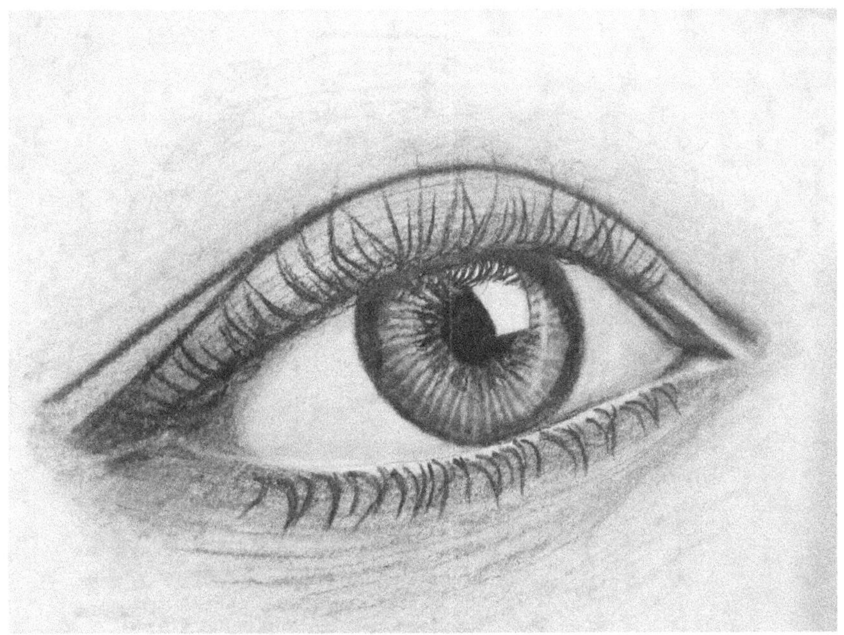

Pencil drawing with a range of values

- Explore the world of contour drawings and blind contour drawings. These are drawings where you make one continuous line and do not pick your pencil tip up off the paper.

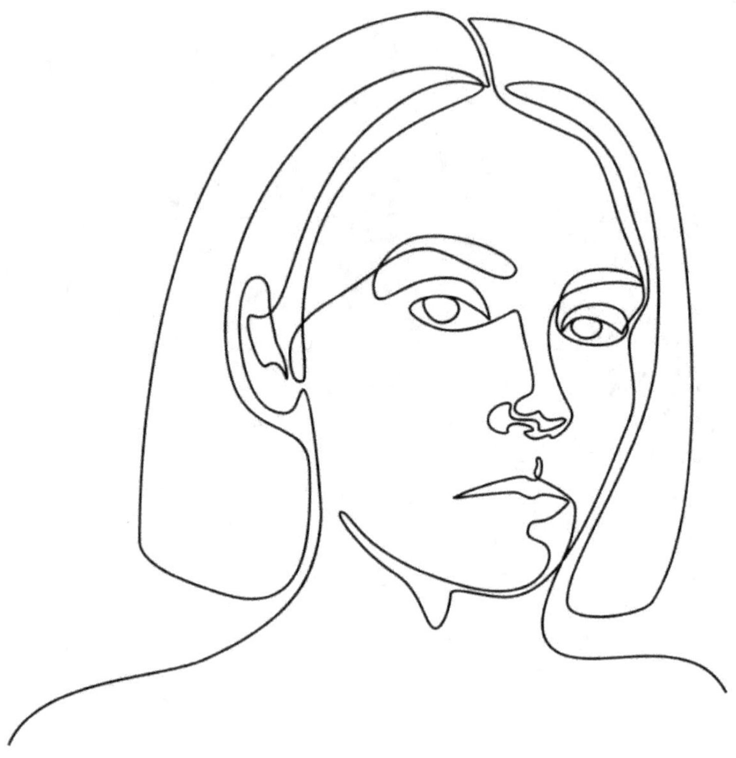

Contour drawing

- Create a zentangle, a picture that uses lines and shapes to create patterns and intricate designs.
- Create a self portrait. Repeat this every so often and see how you have progressed or your style has changed over a period of time.
- Buy a colorless blender and practice blending colors together.
- Create a colored pencil or pastel drawing on black paper.
- Use two or three of these materials together. For example, color

with color pencil, add detail lines with pen, maybe even add some dramatic effects with small bits of marker.

· Practice blending with the pastels and create a landscape. Impressionist paintings are good examples to use for reference images.

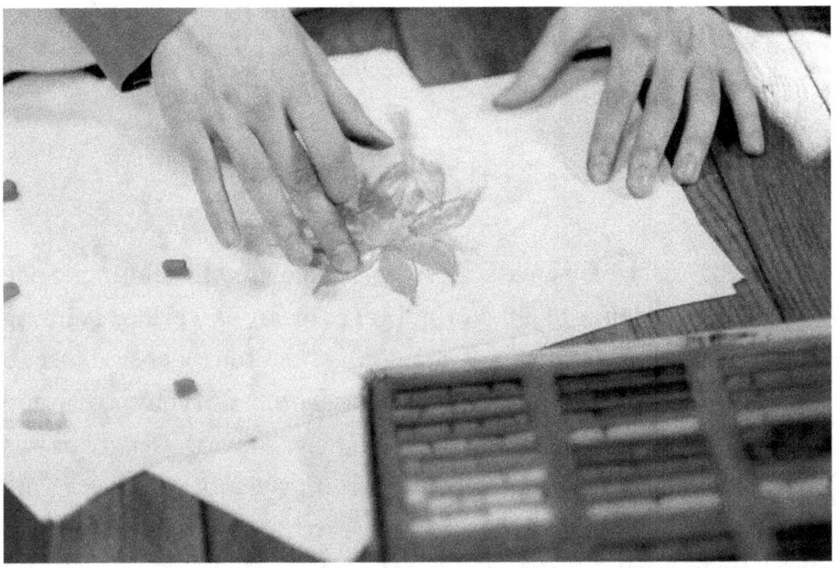

Chalk pastel drawing

· See how many days in a row you can draw in your sketchbook. Can you dedicate 10, 15 or 30 minutes everyday to drawing for a week, a month?

6

Painting

Most of you have already experimented with painting, if not, it is time to jump in and get as messy as you like. Painting can be relaxing, if you don't stress too much and just go with the flow. There are a few different types of paint you can use and many different painting styles. Unfortunately, due to the length of this book, I will not go into depth about different styles of painting. If you are really into painting, check out famous artists and art movements to expand your knowledge of various painting styles. Below are different types of paints, pros and cons of each, along with some exercises to get you painting.

Tempera Paint

If you painted when you were a child, you most likely used tempera paint because it is washable. Elementary and even middle school art teachers use tempera paint for this reason along with its lower price point and wide availability. You can find tempera paint in most stores from Target to Michael's and on Amazon. However, tempera paint is thinner than the other options which means you might need multiple coats to get a solid color. It also is hard to cover up a darker color with a lighter color due to its thinness.

Acrylic Paint

As you grow in your artistic ability, it is worth upgrading your tempera paints for acrylic paints. They have a thicker body which provides a solid coat of color and allows for easy blending. However, they tend to be more expensive than tempera paint and do not always wash out of your clothing (sometimes I have luck washing out acrylic paint, other times I haven't) so wear an apron.

Oil Paint

Unless your parents are artists, you have a proper art studio space, or are taking art classes, you most likely will not be using oil paints at home. Besides being very expensive, they require special chemicals for cleaning (remember how water and oil do not mix, water will not remove oil paint). If you really enjoy painting, oil paints are wonderful to use because of their long drying times allowing you to work on a single painting for much longer than if you were using acrylic paint.

Watercolor Paints

Watercolor paints are available in palettes, which you probably have used as a child, or in liquid form. The palettes are much more cost effective then the liquid form, making it a great addition to your studio space. However, watercolors are much trickier to use than people think. Due to their transparent nature, you cannot cover up paint with another color, plus you use water to dilute the color to create different tints and shades, rather than mixing white or black.

Ink

Ink is similar to watercolor paints, as they are both a water-based media. However, they typically range in black and brown tones (so not bright colors). Ink is a great way to add variety to your drawings or to create richer blacks with your watercolors.

Clean Up

Tempera, acrylic, watercolor, and ink are all water soluble, which means they can be cleaned up with water. As you paint, keep your brushes in a clean cup of water so the paint doesn't dry on the bristles. Acrylic paint is very hard to wash out of the paint brush bristles once it dries; this is the same for clothing. If you get acrylic paint on your clothes, wash the item in cold water immediately. For that reason, wear an old shirt or apron so you don't have to worry. Use a damp rag, cleaning spray, or cleaning wipes to clean your work area. As mentioned before, oil paint needs a special solvent to remove the oil paint from the bristles.

Suggested Activities to Enhance Your Painting Skills

- Using tempera or acrylic paint, practice mixing secondary and intermediate colors.
- Practice mixing tints and shades of a color.
- Practice blending colors together by creating a sunset painting.
- Experiment with different watercolor techniques: dry brush, wet brush on dry paper, wet brush on wet paper, sprinkle salt on top of wet paint to get a reaction, and create gradations (you can find tons of other techniques online or in watercolor books).
- Create an abstract painting.

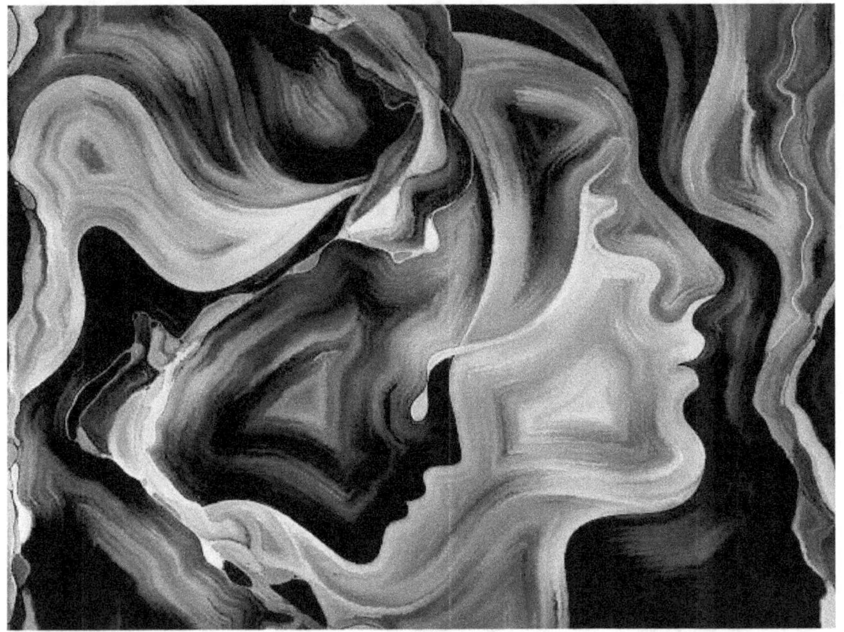

Abstract painting

- Paint a landscape.
- Set up a still life of personal objects to paint.
- Create a watercolor resist painting: draw with a white oil pastel or crayon then add watercolor on top; the oil pastel creates boundaries for the paint (remember, oil and water do not mix).

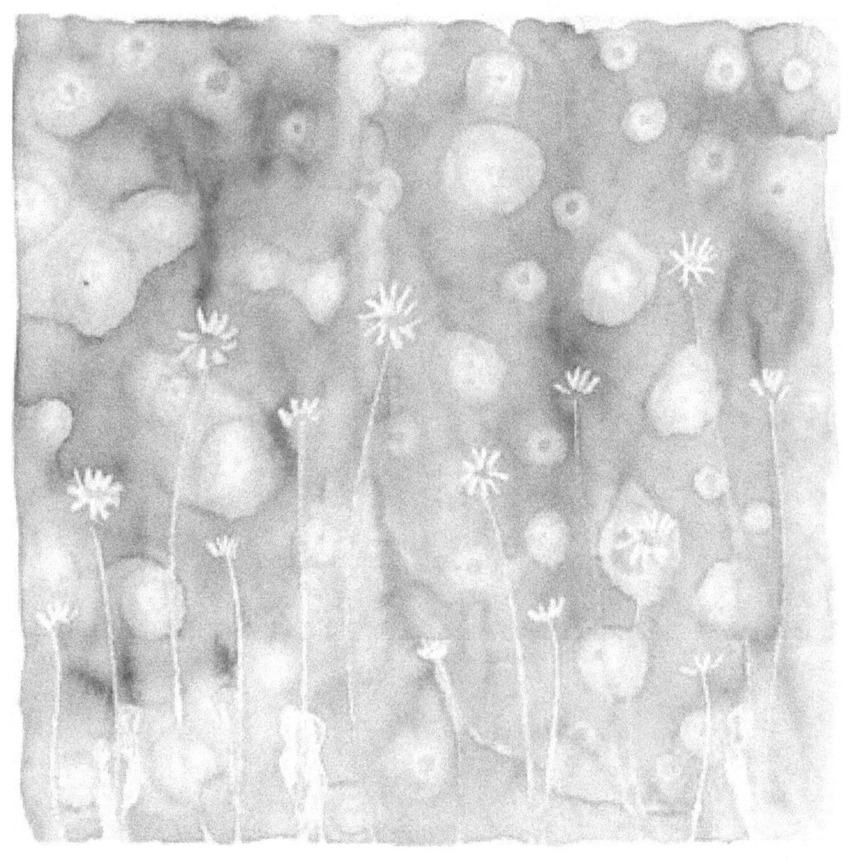

Watercolor resist painting

7

Printmaking

This may be one process you haven't explored before but is one technique that every young artist should experiment with. Printmaking is a process where an artist creates one plate which will be printed multiple times, leaving you with numerous prints. Most of the work is in carving your plate (not all printmaking methods used carved plates). However, once your plate is prepared, you can print 10, 20, or 100 times. This process is great for designs in which you would like multiple prints of the same image, such as holiday cards (get ready to start your art business now).

Even though printmaking may seem like an advanced art making process, there are ways to create your own prints with limited supplies and space. I have included the two printmaking techniques that are the most at-home friendly. If you really enjoy this process you can research more advanced techniques such as intaglio and screen printing. These are not very suitable for at-home printing because they need specific supplies which tend to be more expensive, more space, and are time intensive. However, you may find a local art class that teaches these techniques.

Relief

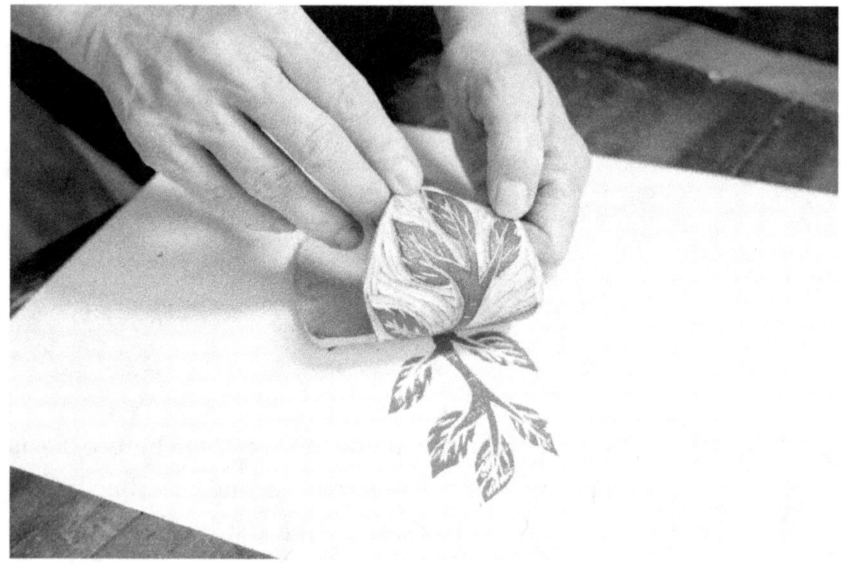

Lino cut relief printmaking

Relief printing is the process of printing from a raised surface where the negative space has been cut away. Woodblocks and linoleum are the two materials typically used for relief printing. However, you can also use Styrofoam plates or trays (repurposed meat trays) for a cheaper alternative. Blick Art Materials carries linoleum in a range of densities based on your skill level. For beginners, a softer piece is preferable. In addition to the material you will be carving, you will also need to purchase a carving tool with a variety of tip sizes, water based printing ink, a brayer (to roll ink onto your plate), multiple sheets of heavy weight paper, and a baren or large wooden spoon (to firmly press to back of the paper during the transferring process).

Mono print

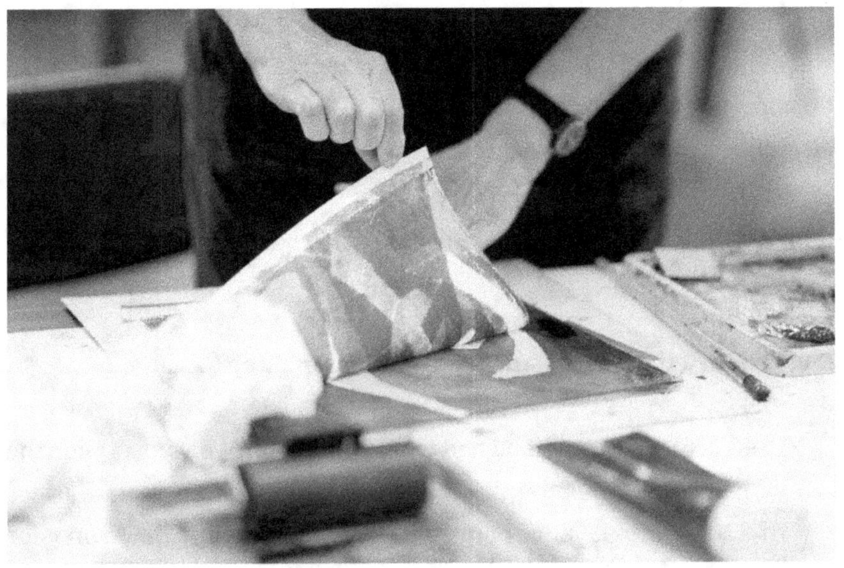

Mono print on Plexiglas

The prefix mono means one. Unlike all other printing processes, no two mono prints are the same because you are not printing from a carved plate. This process is created by painting onto a smooth surface and transferring the image onto your paper. You may have created a mono print when you were younger by applying paint to half of your paper then folding the paper in half and the paint is transferred to the other side.

Clean Up

Unfortunately, printmaking is a messy process. However, that shouldn't be a reason for you to shy away from trying a printmaking project; sometimes the messier the project the more enjoyment it is. By purchasing water soluble ink, the clean up process is nothing more than washing dishes. Thoroughly rinse all materials in cool water. Finish by spraying your work surface with a multipurpose cleaner or using cleaning wipes to wipe down your work area.

Suggested Activities to Enhance Your Printmaking Skills

- Use a scrap piece of wood and wrap yarn around the block. Glue the yarn in place. When the glue is dry, press the block onto a flat surface that has a thin layer of paint. Press the block firmly down on your paper. Repeat the process to create multiple prints.
- Use the bottom of different materials, such as the bottom of a cup, yogurt container, paper towel roll, etc., and dip into paint. Press firmly down onto your paper. Repeat the process to create layers of the prints.
- Take an apple or potato and cut it in half. Then use a knife (with your parents permission) to carve a simple design, like a star. Remember, whatever area you carve away will be the negative space (will not be inked). If you want the star to be printed, you will carve around the shape. Press onto a flat surface that has a thin layer of paint or ink. Press the food firmly down on your paper. Repeat the process to create multiple prints.
- Using a Styrofoam plate or repurposed meat tray, create a simple relief print. Draw your design onto the plate with a pencil or pen.

Press firmly down to ensure that the marks are creating a recessed area. Use a foam roller (can be purchased at any craft store) to roll paint or ink over your plate. Place a sheet of paper on top of the plate and press firmly over the entire area to transfer paint onto your paper.

- Create a table top mono print. Use masking tape to tape an area of your table (or put aluminum foil down if your parents do not want you to put the ink directly onto the table top). Squeeze the ink directly on the table inside your taped area. Use a brayer to spread the ink around. Then draw a design with a pencil, a q-tip, or your finger. Lay your paper on top of the ink and rub to transfer your print to your paper.
- Purchase printmaking supplies (I recommend purchasing through Blick Art Materials) and create your own linoleum print. Draw your design on to your piece of linoleum, carve your design using the carving tools, ink your plate, and print your design. Repeat to get as many prints as desired.

8

Collage and Mixed Media

There is so much to explore when working with collages and mixed media. People tend to stay within the bounds of paper when creating collages but you can add pretty much anything that will stick with glue. Did you just go on a trip and collect photos, tickets, maps, shells, and/or random trinkets along the way? Incorporate those items into a mixed media collage. The key is to use a paper or board that will support the objects you want to use.

Paper

There are so many different kinds of paper you can use for your collage; construction paper, scrapbook paper, tissue paper, magazine pages, newspaper, the list can go on. I suggest keeping old magazines, saving random notes from your BFF, and always look for sales on scrap booking materials when you go to the store.

Glue

You probably have a half dried glue stick hanging around your house somewhere, buy a new one. They are cheap and are great for keeping pieces of paper in place as you collage. I recommend staying away from liquid glue when collaging as they tend to wrinkle the paper. However, a layer of Modge Podge at the end to seal your college is a must. There are some no-name brands that work fine and they come in both matte and glossy.

Unfortunately, there are so many other supplies you could use within your collage, that I am not going to list them out here since I have included a range of items in the supply section of the book. If you like collaging, start a collection of scraps of fabric, photos, notes, stickers, nature, etc. to have at your disposal when creating collages.

Clean Up

I do not know anyone who can work with glue and stay sticky free. Keep a damp cloth at your workstation to wipe off any sticky residue from your fingers as you work. Most of the glue you will use is water soluble, so you can wipe your area with a damp rag or cleaning spray at the end of the working session.

Suggested Activities to Enhance Your Collaging Skills

· Create a collage using different types of paper.

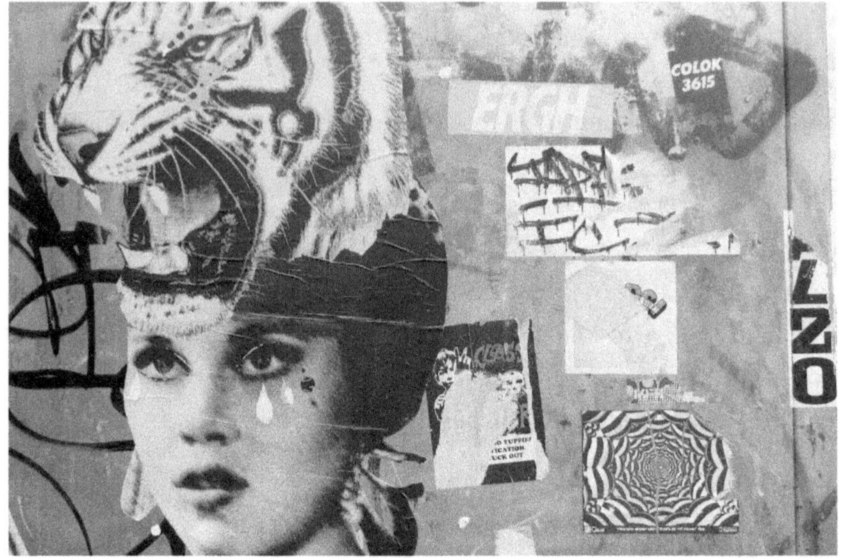

Mixed media collage

- Create a mixed media collage using paper, scraps of fabric, cardboard, or other random materials you have around.
- Collage a simple background, then draw or paint on top of your dried collage.
- Choose a subject matter to collage, such as a flower or a portrait.

9

Sculpture

Sculptures are three-dimensional art forms and can use a wide range of materials. Have you ever made something three-dimensional before, this is anything that takes up space? If you haven't, now is your time to try. The process of creating sculptures is different from drawing or painting because you have to think about all sides of the piece (top, bottom, left, right, inside). You may realize that it is not your preferred method of art making but it is good to experiment. Like collage and mixed media, there are many different materials you can use to create sculptures, I will list a few that you may want to try but think outside the box and use whatever you have on hand.

Sculpting Clay

Play dough, Model Magic, polymer clay, and air dry clay are several different types of sculpting clay you can use at home to create small three-dimensional objects. Hopefully, you have all used play dough, this is great for beginners and if you are on a budget but it doesn't work great for complex sculptures as it dries quickly. Model Magic is another great media for beginners because it's inexpensive, requires very little clean up, has a long drying time, and comes in various colors. Something cool about Model Magic, you can use markers to color the material to expand your color options.

As you advance in your sculpting abilities, try out polymer clay. It is a little tricky to get the hang of working with because you have to knead the material to make it workable. But it comes in a variety of colors and you can bake it in your oven to harden your pieces. However, it is more expensive than the other options. Air dry clay is another material to explore. It is the closest of these materials listed to actual clay and it doesn't need to be fired in a kiln. You can also paint it once it's dry. However, because of the particles in the clay, this is a material you should use in a well vented room and be very thorough in cleaning up any residue (it is basically dust and you don't want to be breathing it in).

Clay

True ceramics is something that you will not be able to do at home unless your parents have access to a kiln (the "oven" that heats the clay to an extremely high temperature). Most kids love playing with clay and if you do as well, find a local pottery shop because they almost always have classes.

Wire

Wire is a material some people don't typically think about using to make art but you can create intricate designs. There are various thicknesses of wire you can buy and overall it is not expensive. The big thing is you will need to buy a pair of wire cutters because your home scissors will not do the trick. Wearing glasses (safety or sunglasses) is also a good idea and it is wise to work in an area where you can easily sweep up any small bits of metal that get flung around from cutting (i.e. not in your bedroom).

Yarn

Knitting and crocheting are two typical yarn creations people make. There are many other ways to use yarn within your artwork. Add it to a collage, create a mobile, weave a basket, cover cardboard, or add it to your clay sculpture. With some liquid glue, yarn will stick to many materials, can add texture, comes in many colors, and is inexpensive.

Cardboard

Are you on a budget and want to build something? Start saving those cardboard boxes from your online orders or your cereal and cracker boxes (paper board). Hot glue is the best to use when working with cardboard as it dries quickly to hold pieces in place. A good pair of scissors, a craft knife, or a box cutter will make your life easier when cutting through corrugated cardboard. If you are using a craft knife or box cutter, make sure you are using a cutting mat to protect the table underneath and be VERY mindful of where your fingers are (this might require you to have adult supervision). Another plus about working with cardboard is that it is a great material if you want to build something large.

Repurposed Objects

Paper towel rolls, plastic containers, wooden sticks, old toys, you name it, it can probably be used to create a sculpture in some way. Even if you aren't on a budget, thinking about how you might be able to use random objects that aren't being used in your life anymore is a great way to use your creative thinking skills and reduce waste.

Clean Up

Sculpting clay will require a little more clean up as some products will leave a residue. However, you only need a wet rag or cleaning wipes and a little elbow grease to ensure your area is clean. Make sure all wire pieces are swept up because you do not want to step on a tiny metal shard. Yarn, cardboard, and repurposed objects need to be swept up at the end of your working session.

Suggested Activities to Enhance Your Sculpting Skills

- Use sculpting clay to create a cartoon character.
- Create a realistic food item using sculpting clay.

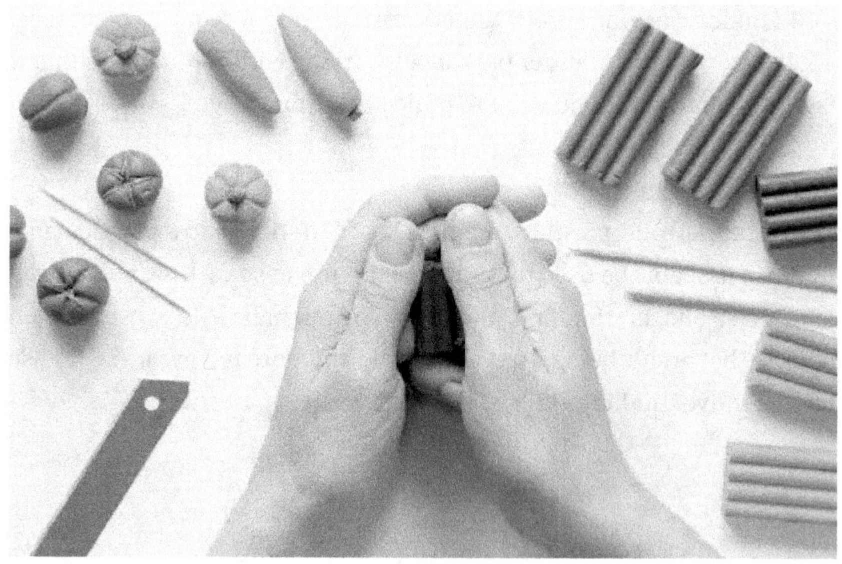

Polymer clay

- Use wire and make an animal.
- Make an abstract cardboard wall hanging.
- Make a life size sculpture out of cardboard.

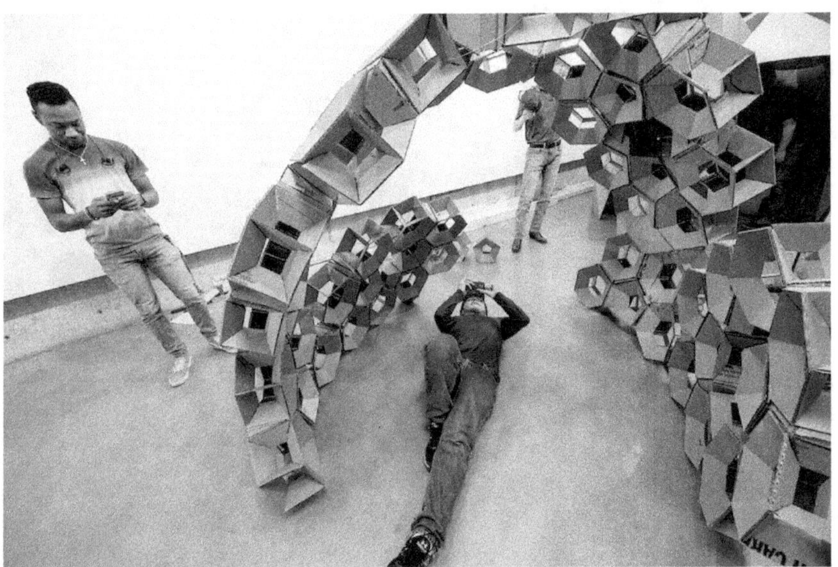

Cardboard sculpture

- Collect random objects and create a mixed media sculpture using at least three different materials.

10

Art Vocabulary

Abstract - artwork that does not represent an accurate depiction of reality

Analogous colors - colors that are next to each other on the color wheel

Background - the part of the picture that seems to be the farthest away

Balance - the visual effect of equality; there are three types of balance: symmetrical balance, asymmetrical balance, and radial balance

Color - a phenomenon of light; the appearance of an object described in terms of hue, brightness, and saturation

Color scheme - a grouping of colors based on their relationship to each other on the color wheel

Color wheel - a tool for organizing colors

Complementary colors - colors across from each other on the color wheel

Composition - the arrangement of the elements of art and the principles of design within a work of art

Contrast - refers to the differences between elements, such as light and dark or large and small shapes

Contour drawing - an outline of the shapes and subject matter

Cool colors - blues, greens, and violets

Cross-hatching - intersecting lines to show value in drawings

Elements of art - the building blocks of any artwork; line, shape, value, color, texture, form, and space are the seven elements of art

Emphasis - when special attention or importance is placed on one area or object through color, line, shape, size, contrast and/or detail

Focal point - the part of the composition with the greatest emphasis

Foreground - the part of the picture that appears closest to the viewer

Form - a three-dimensional object that takes up space

Geometric shapes - shapes that follow a specific formula, such as a square (will always have four equal sides)

Hatching - parallel lines that indicate value in drawings

Intermediate colors - colors created when a primary and secondary color are mixed; such as blue-green, red-orange; also called tertiary colors

Line - a path of a moving point

Mixed media - artwork that uses more than one material

Monochromatic - a color scheme that uses one color and tints and shades of that color

Movement - the visual effect of motion, such as an animal running, or the visual flow of an artwork for the viewer's eyes to travel

Negative space - the area of space around the subject matter

Organic shapes - irregular shapes that are often found in nature

Perspective - a system of representing three-dimensional objects on a two-dimensional surface giving the illusion of depth

Positive space - the subject matter within the composition

Primary colors - cannot be mixed by any other color; red, blue, and yellow

Principles of design - contrast, balance, emphasis, proportion, rhythm, movement, variety, and unity help the artist organize the elements of art into a visually pleasing work of art

Proportion - the size relationship between parts of a whole

Realistic - artwork that attempts to recreate the likeness of the subject matter

Rhythm - the suggestion of movement or action through the use of repeating lines, shapes, colors or other elements

Secondary colors - produced when two primary colors are mixed together: green, orange, and violet

Self-portrait - a portrait of himself

Shade - when black is added to darken a color

Shape - a two-dimensional area clearly set off by one or more of the other visual elements

Space - the area around, above, below, between, and within things

Still life - artwork that shows inanimate objects

Subject matter - what an artwork depicts

Texture - the way something feels or looks to feel if touched

Three-dimensional - artwork that has length, width, and depth, such as sculptures

Tints - when white is added to lighten a color

Tones - when gray is added to a color

Two-dimensional - artwork that has length and width, such as paintings and photographs

Unity - the idea that all parts of the artwork are cohesive and appear complete

Value - the lightness or darkness of an object; the gradual change from white to black

Variety - the different elements used within an artwork

Warm colors - reds, oranges, and yellows

11

Conclusion

Hopefully, this book has provided you with knowledge so you are comfortable in creating an art studio at home. This, by no means, is a complete reference, it is meant to guide you in the beginning stages of your artistic journey. It should open your eyes to new materials that are easily accessible for you to try at home. Unfortunately, I was not able to include full length art lessons but as you experiment and find your preferred methods of making, look for art projects online or through other books. Maybe one day, I will have a project based book.

Until that day, if this book was useful, I would greatly appreciate you writing a review on Amazon.

Resources:

Amazon. (n.d.). Amazon. https://amazon.com

BLICK Art Materials. (n.d.). Dick Blick Art Supplies. https://www.dickblick.com/

Hobby Lobby Arts & Crafts Stores. (n.d.). Hobby Lobby. https://www.hobbylobby.com

Ingram, C. (2018, October 26). *The ultimate collection of elements of art examples and definitions.* Art Class Curator. https://artclasscurator.com/elements-of-art-examples/

Ingram, C. (2018, November 17). *The ultimate collection of principles of design examples and definitions.* Art Class Curator. https://artclasscurator.com/principles-of-design-examples/

KET Education. (2019, October 4). Visual Arts Glossary - KET Education. https://education.ket.org/resources/visual-arts-glossary/

Michaels. (n.d.). Michaels. https://www.michaels.com

Nyberg, J. (2022, September 17). *15 art techniques every kid should try.* Art Makes People. https://artmakespeople.com/art-techniques-every-kid-should-try/

Printmaking Techniques. (n.d.). Pace Prints. https://paceprints.com/techniques

Schukei, A. (2023). 5 different ways to try monoprinting in the art room. The Art of Education University. https://theartofeducation.edu/2017/10/5-different-ways-to-try-monoprinting-in-the-art-room/

Target. (n.d.). Target. https://www.target.com

Walmart. (n.d.). Walmart. https://www.walmart.com